HISTORIC VEHICLES IN MINIATURE

HISTORIC VEHICLES IN MINIATURE
The Genius of Ivan Collins

Revised and Expanded

OREGON HISTORICAL SOCIETY PRESS • Portland

Introduction & Annotation by Ron Brentano

Foreword by Ivan L. Collins

Special Note by Mrs. Laura Collins

FRONTISPIECE • OHS NEG. NO. OrHi 23855

Ivan Collins was justifiably proud of the craftsmanship (many would say artistry) he brought to his work. He eventually completed 62 miniature vehicles. In this photograph taken in the 1940s, he poses with his work up to that point.

The remarkable Collins Collection came to the Oregon Historical Society through the generous interest of Mrs. Ivan (Laura) Collins and the equally generous financial support of Maurie Clark of Portland, Oregon.

This book would be not have been possible without the skill and thoughtful attention of the following past and present members of the Oregon Historical Society staff: Maurice Hodge—the former head of the OHS photo lab who did the photography for the previous edition of this book; Evan Schneider—who added his expertise to the project with splendid detail photography; David Gillaspie—who handled the wagons and helped to keep the photo shoots running smoothly; Marsha Matthews—who allowed protective access to the collections; Mikki Tint—for assisting with photography scheduling; and Virginia Linnman—who helped imagine a beautiful new publication.

The Oregon Historical Society also extends a thank you to Hiawatha Johnson for his work on conserving and cleaning the Ivan Collins Collections, to Don Hunter for offering his warm memories of working with Ivan Collins, and to Bernie McTigue at the University of Oregon Library Special Collections for permission to reprint the Ivan Collins Introduction.

Oregon Historical Society Press • 1200 SW Park Avenue • Portland, OR 97205 • www.ohs.org

Library of Congress Cataloging in Publication Data

© Oregon Historical Society

Historic vehicles in miniature
Catalog of the Oregon Historical Society's Ivan Collins Collection
Bibliography: p.
Includes index
1. Collins, Ivan 1906-1971—Art Collections—Catalogs—. 2. Wagons—Models—Private Collections—Oregon—Portland—Catalogs. 3. Carriages and carts—Models—Private Collections—Oregon—Portland—Catalogs. 4. Oregon Historical Society—Catalogs. I. Brentano, Ron. II. Title. III. Title: Ivan Collins collection.

TS20003.U6P676 1983 688.6′0228 83-16748

Revised expanded edition, 1998
ISBN 0-87595-268-2

The staff of the Oregon Historical Society
dedicates this edition of *Historic Vehicles in Miniature*
to the memory of their friend and co-worker, Ron Brentano.

The Oregon Historical Society would like to thank
the following for their generous support.

Clark Foundation

Wells Fargo

**Bowerman Family Fund
of the Oregon Community Foundation**

The conservation and restoration of objects from the
Oregon Historical Society's collections is made
possible by a generous grant from the

Meyer Memorial Trust

HISTORIC VEHICLES IN MINIATURE
Contents

HISTORIC VEHICLES IN MINIATURE
Contents

HISTORIC VEHICLES IN MINIATURE
Foreword

Ivan L. Collins

Miniaturization is a process older than recorded history. A considerable portion of knowledge of early civilization has been gained from the study of miniatures uncovered in archaeological excavations. Miniatures, if adequately done on a three-dimensional basis, are unequalled as a medium to reflect the past environments in which civilizations have grown.

It is, then, the purpose of this collection of wagons to recapture some of the color and romance of the vehicles of yesteryear; to preserve a visual as well as documentary record of the now rapidly disappearing wagon and the part it played in the development of these United States.

If a miniature is to have any validity as a historical record, it must be created within the same framework of discipline as written history. The line between the actual and the fictional is often very thin, but in neither field can they be allowed to overlap. In the specialized subject of horse-drawn transportation, the temptation to improvise is ever present, especially when the very nature of the work is in itself an improvisation.

Equally important in the historical miniature is legibility. That is, the scale of the miniature must be large enough to permit not only the basic design of the subject, but variations in types of construction, new uses, the advent of new inventions and materials, to be easily understood by the viewer.

The scale used by the Museum of Historic Wagons in Miniature is 1½ inches to the foot, or exactly one-eighth actual size. Thus, a fifth-grade child standing beside a wagon would, in miniature size, be about seven inches tall; a four-foot diameter wheel would be six inches in diameter. This scale permits a record of over fifty types of horse-drawn vehicles to be shown in less space than would be required for two or three full-sized subjects.

A problem which constantly confronts the miniaturist is that the very detailed and technical nature of the work may lead the viewer to become intrigued with intricate bits of minute workmanship to the exclusion of an understanding that such workmanship presents, in perspective, the lost arts of the carriage designer, the wheelwright, and the blacksmith.

If the viewer, as he goes from wagon to wagon, could mentally scale himself down to the wagon size, it would contribute to the realization that *this* is the way our people lived; *these* are the vehicles that carried them west, pushing back frontiers; *these* are the servants that built their roads, hauled lumber for their houses, and took their products to market; *these* are the friends that made their lives gracious and pushed back loneliness. *These* are the creation of American minds and hands that brought this country to the threshold of its greatness.*

---

*Taken from Collins' foreword to "Teacher's Guide to the University of Oregon's Museum of Historic Wagons in Miniature," published with permission of University of Oregon Special Collections. Ivan Collins was director of the Museum from 1965 to 1971.

HISTORIC VEHICLES IN MINIATURE
Introduction

Ron Brentano

L ooking at the reproductions in this volume, it might be difficult to remember that the vehicles presented here are miniatures and not the real thing. All Collins' models were built to one-eighth scale (one-eighth of an inch in the model is equivalent to an inch of the actual vehicle; proportionately, a six-foot-tall man would be scaled down to nine inches). While some of the models may appear surprisingly small (such as the top buggy or the spring sleigh), all are built to the same scale, and their size difference corresponds to that of the actual vehicles. The driver of a mail wagon, for example, generally had to watch his head when entering its approximately four-foot-high body. The freight wagon driver, on the other hand, would have had no trouble; with its six-foot-diameter wheels the vehicle dwarfed passing buggies, much the same as a semi-truck and trailer of today looms over modern cars.

Only two of the models are made of balsawood: the lumber wagon and the covered wagon. Both are lightweight and brittle, and it was for these qualities that Collins considered balsa the least desirable building material. The rest of the models are built of harder, more durable and flexible woods.

Fortunately, many of Collins' construction materials were obtained with the collection, drawer after drawer of miniature parts and tools, nuts, bolts and drills so small they appear to be indistinguish-

During the 19th century, numerous machines and jigs were used for every possible step of wooden wheel making. When these machines became obsolete early in this century they were relegated to the scrap pile. Collins replicated several of these rarely seen devices in one-eighth scale as an aid in assembling the wheels for his carriages. This machine supported the wheel while a heated metal tire was being fitted. The completed wheel was then immediately plunged into a water trough which shrank the tire onto the wooden wheel.

OHS NEG. NO. **OrHi 68031**

able in size until measured with a micrometer. The hand tools include miniature scrapers, spokeshaves, chisels, wrenches, gauges, pliers, surgical clamps and finger and thumb planes. These materials vividly demonstrate Collins' skill and determination in creating the perfect scale model of his collection.

Some of Collins' specially built machines and tools are not only accurately scaled models but were actually used in the construction of the vehicles. For example, for wheel making he built a spoke positioner, a workbench with vises and two other benches for holding wheel parts during assembly; one has a water trough for shrinking the heated tires onto the wheel. All these machines duplicate, in miniature, late 19th- and early 20th-century wheelwrights' equipment. Collins bent the iron tires on a one-eighth-scale tire bender he made especially for model building. This geared device has rollers (adjustable to different diameters according to wheel size) and a hand crank. Most of the other metal parts are brass, a few are aluminum, each piece individually fabricated to scale. Some of the tiny brass screws are standard size, available at hardware stores, but many nuts, bolts and threaded stock were tapped and died to suit a particular model.

Astonishingly, Collins' high standard of excellence prevailed from his very first vehicle (the lumber wagon, built in 1937) to his final achievement (the hose wagon, completed on October 1, 1970). The first wagon is as perfectly and as carefully built as the last!

This hand-cranked, multi-geared device is a scaled-down version of a tire-bending machine that weighed nearly one thousand pounds. Collins' model stands but 14 cm. high. These machines were used to bend the metal tire to the proper diameter for a particular wheel.

Ivan Linus Collins spent over thirty years researching and constructing scale models of the horse-drawn vehicles that were common to America from the mid-19th century through the first two decades of the 20th. Most of the vehicles he built were common to the West, and to Oregon in particular. Born in 1906, Collins lived through the last years of the horse-drawn transportation age. With its demise, he witnessed the destruction of its characteristic vehicles, extensive enough that he would later be unable to locate examples of all of those he wished to draw upon for model building.

Although the collection contains numerous carriages, coaches and sleighs, Collins was more interested in the commercial and everyday work vehicles that he grew up with in eastern Oregon, in the vicinity of The Dalles and Dufur, where he was born. In fact, Collins had first-hand experience with many of the vehicles, and as a youngster learned to drive wagons and teams. Other vehicles were so familiar to his locale or family background that he set out quite early to preserve them in miniature form. These include the

HISTORIC VEHICLES IN MINIATURE

The inner structure of Collins' carriages are built in the same manner as the full-sized originals. Collins built this sample to demonstrate his faithfulness to structural detail. OHS NEG. NO. **OrHi 68031**

his work at the Los Angeles Museum. Shortly thereafter, Paramount Films made a short color movie about Collins and his collection for its "Unusual Occupations" series, which was released nationally in January, 1945. *Life* featured an article on Collins in its April 30, 1945 issue, and Collins was flooded with mail for a month. On July 30, 1945, Universal Films made a short black-and-white film at Collins' home.

The recognition and honor rightly accorded Collins never ceased and was for him a source of inspiration. Feature articles continued in major magazines and newspapers, such as the *New York Sunday News* (May 24, 1943), *Mechanics Illustrated* (1953), *Popular Mechanics* (1954), *Holiday Magazine*, the *New York Times*, *Sunset Magazine* and all manner of regional and local newspapers throughout the West.

Collins faced the problem of the misuse of his art by promoters, who promised all sorts of riches for such schemes as a cross-country tour of department stores, and the use of his carriages as centerpieces at wedding dinners and receptions. In the end, he rejected these offers and spent his days realizing his dream of building a collection of miniature vehicles of unique educational value.

Collins stated his goal for each piece in the collection:

> *That we see it not as a miniature, but see through it into the past and into the lives of those who sweated and toiled and worked with the original from which it was copied.*

covered wagon and buckboard in which Collins' great-grandparents traveled to Oregon in 1850, the lumber wagon and header box with which Collins hauled wheat, the gooseneck dray operated by Collins' father as part of his business in The Dalles, the bundle rack, the hotel omnibus, the wool wagon, the mail wagon, the grain box wagon and a few other common vehicles.

Between 1936 and 1944, Collins managed to construct an astounding collection of thirty-two scale models. Recognition, and an endless stream of publicity, began with a front-page story in the *Los Angeles Times* of April 16, 1944, coincident with the opening of an exhibit of

Collins achieved this goal admirably. And by the time of his death in 1971, he had managed to document and build a collection of sixty-three models, models which represent the diversity of vehicles used during the 19th and early 20th centuries.

This was Ivan Collins special signature block that he used on his wagons. It is usually placed in a spot not readily visible to most viewers—under a wagon box or behind a dash board. The pronouncement at the right was written by Ivan Collins and welcomed visitors when the wagons were at the University of Oregon's Museum of Historic Wagons in Miniature in Eugene.

Pronouncement

*The melodious warning of chiming freight bells swaying
on the shoulders of perspiring teams;*

*The scream of oaken brakes holding back the surge of weight
on a tortuous and twisting grade;*

The colorful, if profane, vernacular of the teamsters;

The rhythmic clack of swinging trace chains;

The contrapuntal "clip-clop" of hooves on pavement;

*The graceful beauty of a perfectly appointed and
"turned out" carriage on promenade;*

*The redolence of hot iron and burning wood
drifting from the carriage shop;*

*The excited preparation around the blacksmith shop
as heavy tires are made ready for shrinking;*

*Patterns in the road as powdered dust flows
in liquid rivulets away from the wagon below;*

*Miniature pyrotechnics piercing the darkness
as iron-shod dray teams clatter over the cobblestones;*

*All these are today but pleasant memories
in the minds of a passing generation.*

HISTORIC VEHICLES IN MINIATURE
Overland Wagons

CONCORD COACH
late 19th century

Length: 52.0cm   Height: 35.0cm
Width: 24.8cm   Tongue: 39.4cm

OHS NEG. NO. OrHi 97233

CONCORD COACH

Built almost entirely by hand at the Abbot-Downing workshop in Concord, New Hampshire, more than 3,500 of these coaches were shipped all over the world. The key to the Concord's success was its "thorough-braces" or multiple leather straps, on which the body of the coach rocked. Their prime function was to act as shock absorbers for the benefit of the teams.

In 1868 a trainload of thirty coaches with two car-loads of harness was shipped to Wells Fargo and Co. in Omaha. These larger Concords, built for the West, weighed about 2,500 pounds and carried nine passengers inside and as many more crowded on top. More than a half ton of baggage and express cargo could be loaded in the front and rear boots.

The model was finished in 1942.

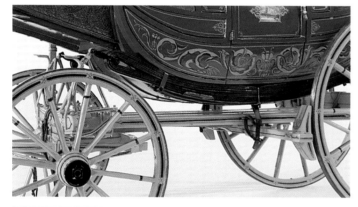

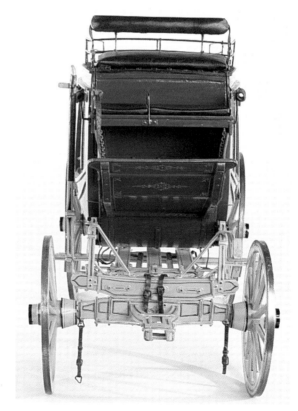

CONESTOGA WAGON
1750-1850

Length: 63.8cm
Width: 25.0cm
Height: 43.0cm

OHS NEG. NO. OrHi 97228

These earliest of American wagons were named for Pennsylvania's Conestoga Valley, where they were built. The valley's craftsmen adapted the graceful and boat-like lines that had first appeared in European vehicles of the 16th and 17th centuries. This design was practical as well as aesthetic; the curved body tended to keep the load at the center of the wagon rather than shifting to the ends, and many feel the shaped body made them easier to move when fording streams.

These wagons were used between the 1750s and 1840s, and could haul ten tons of freight; the six-horse team

and wagon stretched to sixty feet. The drivers rode on one of the horses or walked alongside.

This immaculately detailed model, made in 1939, includes a bucket for hub grease, and a jack, as essential then as they are today. Particular attention has been given to the top, for which, to achieve maximum realism, Collins sought and found a fabric whose thread count came close to one-eighth scale.

ROAD COACH
1835-1917

Length: 48.0cm
Width: 24.2cm
Height: 31.0cm
Tongue: 42.0cm

OHS NEG. NO. OrHi 97231

It was the British who dubbed this type of stage or public coach the "road coach." Customarily, all coaches were named; one of the first to be imported to the United States was named the "Tally Ho," a term later often erroneously applied to almost any vehicle with seats on top. This particular coach was named "Enterprise" and around the turn of the century it operated on regular schedules out of New York.

Pulled by four horses with a "cock horse" to help them up the hills, these ponderous and top-heavy coaches operated successfully on the smoother post roads but failed completely in inland and western roads.

Collins drew the plans for the model from illustrations in the *Manual of Coaching* and *Driving for Pleasure*, both turn-of-the-century classics. The model was completed in 1941.

COVERED WAGON
ca. 1850

Length: 89.0cm   Height: 42.0cm
Width: 25.0cm

OHS NEG. NO. OrHi 97229

COVERED WAGON

This covered wagon and accompanying buckboard are based on ones driven to Oregon by Collins' great-grandparents, Mr. and Mrs. Linus Brooks. Upon arrival in October, 1850, Brooks made the following entry in his diary:

We were six months to a day from the time we left our old home (Beardstown, Illinois) to the day we landed in the (Willamette) Valley. Nothing should be thought too hard for an Oregon emigrant that he can accomplish, saving his life and that of his teems [sic].

This wagon is outfitted with a range of items that might have come across the trail, including chickens in the crate on the side of the wagon, straw ticks, quilts, cooking gear and farm implements. The model was completed in 1937.

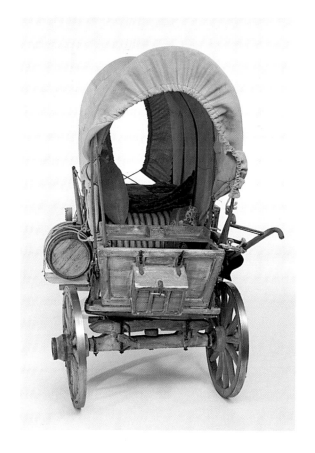

STAGE WAGON

ca. 1850

Length: 84.0cm   Height: 33.6cm
Width: 25.0cm

STAGE WAGON

These light stage wagons carried loads over roads too dangerous for the less rugged Concord coaches. They were called "mud wagons" because of their depend-

ability during inclement weather. Normally, both the Concords and the stage wagons were pulled by six horses; the teams were replaced at each stage station, usually spaced about every twelve miles.

Ben Holladay owned thirty-two of these stages, and in 1860 he sent the first through-stage from Sacramento to Portland clattering up California's Central Valley and over the Siskiyous. It made the trip in the then-unbelievable time of seven days and nights of continuous travel.

The signature block at the upper left can be found under the driver's seat on the back of the dashboard.

The model was completed in 1940.

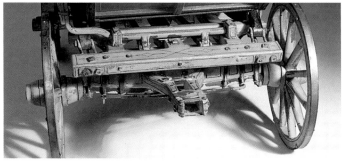

BUCKBOARD
ca. 1850

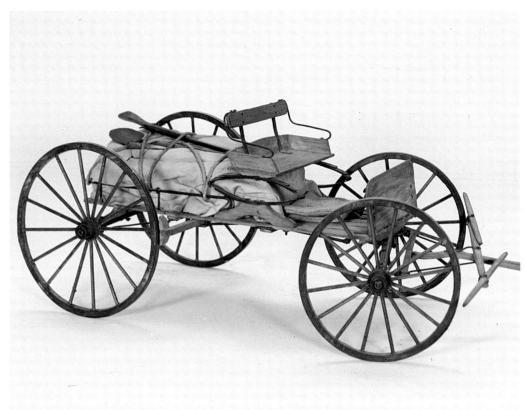

Length: 77.5cm
Width: 21.8cm
Height: 18.0cm

OHS NEG. NO. OrHi 97230

The buckboard was a very utilitarian vehicle around any 19th century working settlement, be it farm, mine or timber camp. Its twentieth century equivalent would be a pick-up truck. Many settlers who made their way west would refit their wagons into buckboards. Collins completed this buckboard in 1939, two years after he had completed the covered wagon.

HISTORIC VEHICLES IN MINIATURE
Farm Wagons

FARM WAGON
1910

Length: 41.5cm
Width: 24.0cm
Height: 29.5cm
Tongue: 45.5cm

OHS NEG. NO. OrHi 97282

This ubiquitous wagon handled almost every kind of hauling job on the farm. Its standard wagon box (shown here) could be lifted off and other kinds of boxes or racks put on instead. Among other things, the boxes carried potatoes, hogs, corn and (as in the case of Oregon's Hood River Valley) boxes of apples. When haying time came, the "hay rack" was used for hauling loads of sweet-smelling hay to the barns. At threshing time "bundle racks" were attached to haul the bundles of ripe grain to the threshing machine. After the grain was threshed,

the original box was put back and loaded with sacks of grain to be hauled to the warehouses and flour mills in nearby towns.

The standard wagon box cost approximately $200, and a set of heavy draft harness cost from $75 to $150.

The model was completed in 1945, and is based on a 1910 wagon by Birdsell Co. of South Bend, Indiana.

RED RIVER CART
ca. 1780-1850

Length: 46.0cm
Width: 21.5cm
Height: 22.8cm

OHS NEG. NO. OrHi 97237

The first carts used in isolated settlements along the Red River of the North were built by french voyageurs and trappers in the late 18th century; their design was later improved by the Scottish colonists. Made of native materials, without a particle of iron or nails, the carts were usually built with only an axe, saw, chisel and auger. No paint, decoration or preservative enhanced these ingeniously contrived carts that supported 800- to 1,400-pound loads. Even the wheels were made without iron tires; instead, they were bound with rawhide over splints to secure the felloes.

Although the carts were generally pulled by a single ox, a horse, a mule or even a milk cow could be used, hitched by a crude rawhide harness. For long hauls, trains (often containing hundreds of wagons) were assembled, with one driver taking care of as many as six carts.

The fertile Red River Valley was plentifully populated by fur-bearing animals including wild buffalo, beaver, otter, mink, fisher, marten, muskrat and fox. At first, carts hauled these hides and furs, and other freight, north to the Hudson's Bay Company's York Factory; later when it became more convenient and profitable to deal with the business concerns of the United States, they headed south.

Collins' model, in the planning stage for twenty years, was completed in 1970.

ORCHARD WAGON

For several decades the thousands of boxes filled with Hood River Valley apples were transported in Orchard Wagons whose small iron wheels permitted use of the low, flat bed, so necessary for orchard work. Farmers usually built the wagon beds to suit their individual requirements, although the bolster springs always had to be purchased.

The iron running gear was assembled and sold by a well-known manufacturer of iron wagons, the Bettendorf Axle Co. of Davenport, Iowa. This firm was one of the first to use vendor-fabricated subassembly parts (made by International Harvester Co., among other firms) and the wheels came from still another company. When not in use in orchard work this wagon was commandeered for other harvesting operations.

Collins made no working drawing for this model; because of the close proximity of an actual wagon to Collins' home in Eugene, Oregon, he made frequent visits and sketches instead of his normal detailed plans. (As of 1965, the original wagon from which Collins made his model was still being used in the Springfield, Oregon, area to haul irrigation pipe.)

Preliminary drafting began April 17, 1965, and the model wagon and load were completed by July 15, 1965. Collins designed the wagon bed and rear step and chose the color to resemble his father's orchard wagon in Dufur, Oregon.

ORCHARD WAGON
late 19th century

Length: 42.0cm Height: 25.8cm
Width: 21.0cm Tongue:46.5cm

OHS NEG. NO. OrHi 97268

GRAIN BOX
WAGON
ca. 1900

Length: 56.0cm
Width: 24.0cm
Height: 28.0cm
Tongue: 44.6cm

OHS NEG. NO. OrHi 97283

Although few exist today, hundreds of these wagons once crowded the roads of eastern Oregon, hauling wheat from thresher to railroad. They were pulled by four to six horses or mules and were unloaded at the grain elevators by raising the front end and opening a gate at the rear. Load capacity of the thirteen-foot-long box was 125 bushels (approximately four tons). The coved-joint pine sides on fir flooring supported by oak sills, all heavily ironed and secured with over 250 bolts, made grain-tight boxes capable of withstanding the jolts and twists of the roughest roads.

The original of this wagon's box was built by F. S. Gunning, a local blacksmithing firm in The Dalles, Oregon. The running gear was factory-built by Mitchell,

Lewis and Co. of Racine, Wisconsin, and distributed by the subsidiary firm of Mitchell, Lewis & Staver of Portland, Oregon. The latter's former building in southeast Portland still stands, freshened with a new coat of paint. In 1998, between SE 1st and 2nd and Morrison and Belmont, a ghost of the phrase "Wagons STUDE-BAKER Carriages" could still be seen near the roof.

Collins made field notes and measurements from a grain wagon found at the Merril Adkisson ranch near Dufur, Oregon, in August 1965, and completed the model in 1966.

Length: 56.5cm
Width: 36.8cm
Height: 24.5cm

OHS NEG. NO. OrHi 97284

On small ranches, grain was usually harvested with a binder, a machine that cut and tightly bound it. The bundles, piled high and stacked like cord wood, were hauled from field to threshing machine in racks mounted on a standard wagon running gear. After the harvest season the racks were stored on trestles and the running gear, with a different box, was available to haul the threshed grain to the railroad.

Most racks were farm built, as was the original from which Collins made his model, found at the E. M. Burtner ranch in Dufur, Oregon. Nuts and bolts and ironwork were available at the nearest blacksmith shop. Much to Collins' surprise, the original had no brake. He added one to his model, fashioned after a brake he helped his father put on their new bundle rack around 1920.

The model was built in 1966.

SHEEPHERDER'S WAGON

ca. 1910

Length: 82.0cm Height: 40.5cm
Width: 24.0cm

OHS NEG. NO. OrHi 97226

SHEEPHERDER'S WAGON

This style of sheepherder's wagon was constructed around 1910 by the Sidney Stevens Implement Co. of Ogden, Utah. The sturdy hardwood and iron-reinforced bodies could be ordered either in kit form or factory assembled; depending on accessories, it cost between $550 and $650.

Included in the model are cans of food (with labels, of course), pots, pans, silverware, bedding, magazines and even a calendar dated June, 1912—all executed in one-eighth scale! Collins' friend, Don Hunter, did the miniaturization for the cans, the booklet and calendar.

Collins drew the plans for this model in 1968 from a wagon once owned by Mrs. Clara Howard of Klamath Falls, Oregon. (Mrs. Howard's grandfather taught Collins to drive a six-horse team.) The wagon is now preserved in the Klamath County Museum in Klamath Falls.

WOOL WAGON
ca. 1890

Length: 52.5cm
Width: 24.5cm
Height: 31.0cm
Tongue: 39.8cm

OHS NEG. NO. OrHi 97286

Although wool-shipping sacks (which hold from twenty-one to twenty-five fleeces and when filled weigh between three hundred and five hundred pounds) have not changed, the method of hauling them has.

Prior to trucking transport, wool was hauled from outlying ranches to the railroads with at least one trailer and frequently two, and with sixteen- or eighteen-head of horses in the harness. The trip often required a week's hot and dusty travel.

This wagon replicates a Studebaker Ranch Wagon with California Rack. The sideboards were ranch made with poles bolted along the top to prevent tears in the sacks. The model, based on the type of wagon used in eastern Oregon, was completed in 1937; it is the second wagon Collins made.

HEADER BOX
1912

Length: 69.2cm
Width: 43.2cm
Height: 33.5cm
Tongue: 45.6cm

OHS NEG. NO. OrHi 97287

The jaunty lines of the header box were developed to allow a wagon to be driven alongside the moving "header"—a wheat harvester that cut the grain, and, by means of a conveyor belt, loaded it into the wagon. When filled, a wagon was driven away to be unloaded at the threshing machine. An empty wagon, following behind, moved into place and the harvesting went on.

For stability on the steep slopes of western wheat fields, the header box's rear axle had a nine-foot track. Four-horse (or mule) teams pulled them; a driver and a man with a pitchfork made up the crew on each. Thousands were used throughout the West, most of them built in local blacksmith shops. In some areas these rigs had no brakes.

In July 1956, Collins found this one at Wayne Sigman's ranch in Dufur, Oregon, and completed the model the following year.

FREIGHT WAGON

Pioneers and their wagon trains opened the roads to the West. These settlers soon needed sugar, salt and coffee, and over the new roads big freight wagons piled high with food and supplies came to their rescue. Loads of cowhides were sent back in the wagons, which creaked and groaned as teams of ten to twenty mules or horses pulled them across the deserts and mountains.

These outfits, with a load capacity of ten tons each, were usually operated by two men; the driver, riding the wheel horse and controlling the teams with a "jerk-line" to the lead horse, and the swamper, who clambered back and forth from wagon to wagon setting brakes. The extra double trees were used when the wagon became stuck, and an extra team could be added to extract the rig.

Collins found this wagon at the Pony Express Museum in Arcadia, California, in 1938, and spent about two-and-one-half months constructing the model. (Work on the accompanying equipment was as demanding and time-consuming as that on the model.)

FREIGHT WAGON
1880-1910

Length: 75.0cm Height: 44.3cm
Width: 24.2cm Tongue: 47.7cm

OHS NEG. NO. OrHi 97282

HISTORIC VEHICLES IN MINIATURE
City Wagons

HOTEL OMNIBUS
ca. 1880

Length: 85.1cm   Height: 36.8cm
Width: 30.5cm

HOTEL OMNIBUS

I n the late 19th century, the Umatilla House was a famous hotel in The Dalles, Oregon. It stood for years at the gateway of the Columbia Basin, bringing champagne, cut glass and a taste of gracious living to a pioneer country of saddles, dust and whiskers. Stopping overnight in The Dalles, it was hard to resist the invitation of the jaunty vehicle and its promise of the hotel's luxury and comfort.

The hotel's bus was built about 1880 in a The Dalles carriage shop by August Wintermeier, a pioneer wagon maker, who patterned it after a typical public carrier used before the advent of the horse car.

In contrast to the more garish advertisements in our buses today, fifteen landscape paintings executed by the local artist R. A. Lauer adorned this vehicle's interior above the windows.

In 1941, while drafting the R.F.D. mail wagon, Collins discovered this bus in the shed near the Fort Dalles' Surgeon's Quarters in The Dalles. With his father, he returned to take measurements the following year and completed the model in 1943.

LUMBER
WAGON
ca. 1895

Length: 49.0cm
Width: 25.0cm
Height: 30.0cm
Tongue: 36.5cm

OHS NEG. NO. OrHi 97250

This is the first wagon Ivan Collins built from scratch. It is a copy, reconstructed from memory, of one of the wagons used on the Collins ranch in eastern Oregon. Collins recorded the details in his notes:

My memory of details of the running gear were supplemented by catalogues from the Los Angeles Heavy Hardware store. The body was built entirely from memory. It was a standard 12 foot bed. Upon close examination by my father, who knew the original wagon even better than I, no errors or deviations could be found. The running gear of the original was by Mitchell, Lewis (Co.), and the original body was built by E. M. Hill, blacksmith at Dufur, Oregon. About 1912 I remember helping burn the irons off the old body and building a new one. I drove

this wagon all the years I was on the ranch and hauled wheat with it, using six horses and pulling a trailer. This type of body, called the California body, was used for all types of hauling throughout the Northwest. The wagon was equipped with staked side boards which could be used for bulk hauling. Most ranchers in the Northwest had a set of high slatted boards that were used to haul 16 inch wood... This one was in the heavy duty class and could haul approximately 7000 pounds or two to three thousand board feet of green lumber.

The model was built as a birthday present for my father. It was completed in January 1937 and sent to my father with a load of cigars. The load of lumber was added later.

MILK WAGON
1912

Length: 33.5cm
Width: 21.5cm
Height: 31.5cm
Tongue: 35.0cm

The internal combustion engine will never compete with horses when it comes to remembering established routes—from door-to-door and back-and-forth across the streets the animals would weave, hesitating to let the delivery men catch up, or refusing to move if a customer was forgotten.

Several manufacturers specialized in these wagons. Together with side-line output of the major wagon companies, the manufacture of delivery wagons constituted a major portion of the wagon industry. In 1912, the average price for this type of wagon was $75.

"Clover Leaf" was a popular name for dairies throughout the country.

The model was completed in 1944 and is based on a wagon owned by 20th Century Fox.

HOOK-AND-LADDER TRUCK
1880

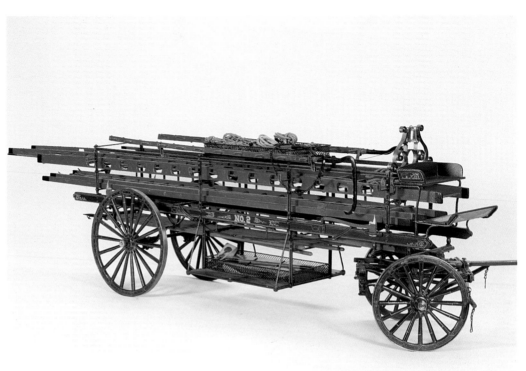

Length: 128.0cm
Width: 23.3cm
Height: 30.7cm

OHS NEG. NO. OrHi 97246

This truck was originally operated by the Chicago Fire Department after 1880, and it typically carried (among other equipment) the following:

24-foot extension ladder
20-foot extension ladder
16-foot bridging ladder
18-foot straight ladders (2)
16-foot roof ladders (2)
140-foot Pompier ladders (2)
100-foot drag rope
Life net
Battering rams
Pull-down hooks and poles

Flood lamp
Fire axes
Bars
Shovels
Door openers

With the change-over to motorized fire equipment, most trucks of this type were destroyed. However, many larger horse-drawn aerial ladder trucks were converted to motor-driven equipment.

Collins based the model, completed in 1940, on an original owned by 20th Century Fox.

Length: 82.3cm
Width: 25.3cm
Height: 40.0cm

OHS NEG. NO. OrHi 97259

Before the days of television commercials and neon signs, and before the development of color printing, one of the principal advertising mediums was the business wagon. Delivery wagons often served the dual purpose of utility and traveling advertisement, but many firms whose services did not require the use of a wagon operated attractive and colorfully decorated vehicles solely to bring their service or product to the attention of the public.

One of the basic principles of advertising—the repetitive presentation of a name, idea or service in a tasteful and elegant manner—found ideal application in the business wagons. Elegance of vehicle became associated with elegance of product, and, as a result, many vehicles were designed, decorated and ornamented quite beyond their utilitarian requirements.

The model was completed in 1956 and is based on a wagon built by Hoeptner and Co. of New York.

HOSE WAGON
1896

Length: 85.2cm Height: 28.8cm
Width: 23.4cm

HOSE WAGON

This is a particularly good example of the artistry, craftsmanship and engineering skill that made the J. and W. Jung Co. of Sheboygan, Wisconsin, a major producer of fine vehicles in the Great Lakes area.

Manufactured for the Sheboygan Fire Department, this Hose Wagon served until replaced by motorized equipment in 1928. The two-horse rig carried a driver, three firemen and up to 1,200 feet of two-and-one-half-inch hose. Its function was to lay hose lines from hydrant to fire, or, on large fires, from the steam pumper to the fire.

This is the last wagon Collins made; he completed it on October 1, 1970. It is based on the original owned by Wesley W. Jung of Sheboygan.

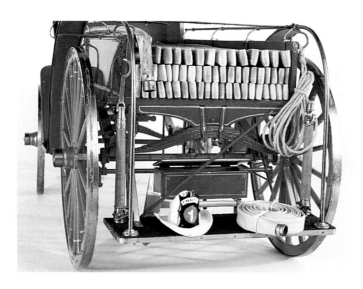

DUMP WAGON
ca. 1898

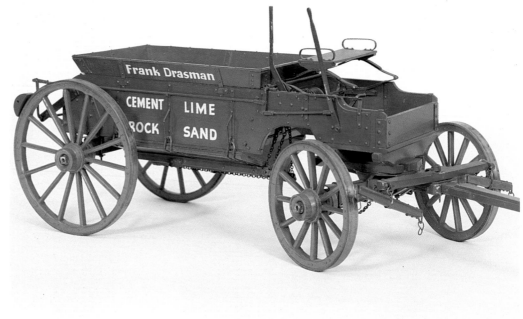

Length: 49.5cm
Width: 24.0cm
Height: 24.9cm
Tongue: 43.2cm

OHS NEG. NO. OrHi 97252

It takes time to empty wagonloads of dirt or sand with shovels; wagons like this one expedited the dumping process. By pedal, doors on the bottom were opened and the load dropped. Cranked shut by a lever-operated winch near the driver's seat, the doors could then be closed as he quickly drove away.

These wagons were used on excavation and earth-moving operations as well as for hauling building materials. In fleets, they hauled dirt from the excavations for the first skyscrapers, while others brought in tons of sand and gravel for the foundations. They dumped dirt and rock along river levees to help hold back the floods, and in some coastal cities they brought loads for landfill.

Dump wagons were made by most wagon manufacturers. This one was built by the Bain Wagon Co., one of the most popular wagon firms in its time.

The model was completed in March of 1945.

ROLL-OFF LUMBER WAGON
ca. 1910

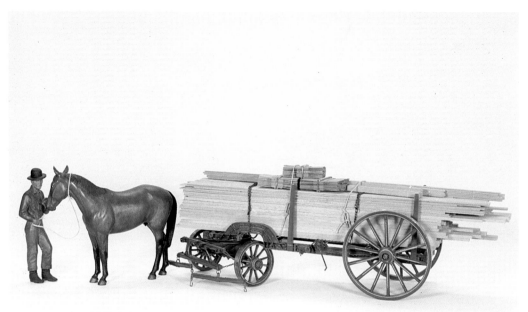

Length: 65.4cm
Width: 22.5cm
Height: 23.8cm

OHS NEG. NO. OrHi 97251

This wagon, developed by A. Streich and Brothers. Co. of Oshkosh, Wisconsin, possessed one of the first mechanical devices for unloading lumber. The company's catalog explained this advantage: *Wagons are so low down one man can put a large load on alone.... A 14-year-old boy can roll a large load on or off with ease.... It dumps the load and leaves it piled on the ground just as it was loaded on the wagon.* This feat was accomplished with rollers whose bearings eliminated friction on the loading surface. Two of the five rollers were connected to a hand crank that could be locked to prevent accidental unloading.

Records concerning this project provide some indication of the effort Collins devoted to model construction; it is one of the few cases where he documented his time and expenses. By the time this model was completed in 1965, Collins had spent about 407 hours on construction, research and field trips; expenses came to $1,965, plus materials!

SPRINKLER
WAGON
ca. 1910

Length: 44.0cm
Width: 24.0cm
Height: 33.0cm
Tongue: 42.1cm

OHS NEG. NO. OrHi 97253

This model is based on a Studebaker-built wagon used in Klamath Falls, Oregon. Since the main portion of that town was built on what used to be the lake's shore, in the summer the dust was so thick that the streets required continuous watering. (After Klamath Falls started paving its streets, about 1910, the dust problem lessened.)

Collins located this wagon at the Klamath County Museum; he then researched technical details at the Smithsonian Institution. After spending seven months on construction, Collins completed the model in 1970.

BREWERY WAGON
1865-1915

Length: 52.5cm
Width: 28.0cm
Height: 40.0cm
Tongue: 46.0cm

OHS NEG. NO. OrHi 97266

These specially adapted wagons hauled kegs of beer from brewery to tavern, or to the bottler. Attached to the bottom of these wagons, between the front and rear wheels, were hooks for hauling more kegs. The umbrella added a flamboyant touch that rarely failed to delight even the most jaded onlooker.

While demand for bottled beer increased in the late 19th century, the federal tax structure made it difficult for brewers to put beer directly into bottles. The beverage first had to be placed in kegs and then transported to the bottler. Many brewers, discouraged by this costly and time-consuming process, had someone else bottle their products until new laws, passed in 1890-91, enabled the brewer to pipe beer directly from the brewhouse to the bottling plant.

Collins completed this model in 1941.

EXPRESS WAGON
1918

Length: 54.0cm
Width: 28.5cm
Height: 40.2cm

OHS NEG. NO. OrHi 97258

The express business in America had its beginning just ten years before the California Gold Rush, when, as a convenience to his neighbors, a conductor on a Boston railroad began carrying parcels between towns and cities on his run. The service became popular, and companies soon formed to operate between important towns and cities throughout the country. Adams Express was one of the first of these companies.

In 1918, when the government took over the railroads, the express companies merged as American Railway Express. In 1920 the railroads and express companies were returned to their owners and the unified express company continued independent operations for nine years. In 1929 the class 1 railroads purchased the business and equipment, and the Railway Express Agency was formed, which stayed in business until 1975.

Collins drafted this wagon in Los Angeles, California, and finished the model in 1947.

FUEL WAGON
early 20th century

Length: 41.5cm
Width: 23.0cm
Height: 30.0cm
Tongue: 44.5cm

OHS NEG. NO. OrHi 97257

The sight of wagons hauling wood for stoves and furnaces was common in the Northwest. Not equipped with a braking mechanism, these wagons were controlled by means of special harness (often called a "britchen harness") and the unusual double-neck yoke. The box and crank-operated dumping mechanism were blacksmith built; the running gear of this rig, a Weber mountain wagon manufactured by McCormick-Deering Co., featured a patented fifth wheel and swivel reach that provided flexibility and stability on uneven roads.

From 1900 to 1928, Portland's Holman Transfer Co. operated two hundred of these vehicles.

Collins drafted the plans for the model from the last Holman wagon, which he found in Shaniko, Oregon. He completed the model in 1969.

HEARSE
1830

Length: 49.0cm Height: 29.0cm
Width: 21.5cm Tongue: 41.7cm

HEARSE

With its gleaming silver and plate glass, flowing plumage and intricate carving, the finest black horses and a liveried driver, the hearse represented a solemn but dignified final triumph, and thereby comforted those left behind.

The model is inspired by a hearse built by the Ohio firm of Sayers and Scoville. One of the finest examples of the hearse-designer's art, it possessed a fineness of line and an artistic balance seldom seen in a vehicle of this type. The pure Corinthian columns and the recurrent motif of the fleur-de-lis were obviously executed by highly skilled artists and carvers.

Plans for the model were drafted from a hearse found in Eugene, Oregon, in 1941. The model was completed in 1942 after a little over three months' work, which included casting and plating the finials and building a coffin.

ICE WAGON
1895

Length: 75.2cm
Width: 24.2cm
Height: 31.0cm

OHS NEG. NO. OrHi 97256

In horse-drawn days, ice to be sold commercially was either frozen in one hundred- to three hundred-pound cakes or sawed from frozen rivers and lakes. Ice wagons then carried these cakes to customers, where purchases were cut to order and weighed on scales on the back of the wagon.

Ice wagons were always popular with children. At every stop these wagons were surrounded by droves of delighted youngsters scrambling for bits of ice, and maybe even a brief ride.

Notes for the model, which was completed in 1947, were taken from a wagon located at Rancho El Providencia in Los Angeles, California.

R.F.D. MAIL WAGON

ca. 1900

Length: 57.0cm
Width: 21.5cm
Height: 16.9cm

OHS NEG. NO. OrHi 97261

In 1896 the U.S. Post Office Department introduced the Rural Free Delivery (R.F.D.) System so that farm dwellers could receive their mail every day, a service already provided to residents of towns and cities. Until that time it sometimes would be weeks or more before farmers could get to town to pick up letters and newspapers. In wagons built especially for their use, mail carriers were soon jogging along the country roads.

This one-horse wagon was probably made by Ligonier Carriage Co. of Ligonier, Indiana, which specialized in mail wagons. The driver sat cozily inside, guiding the horse with reins through the open front window. During the winter the reins passed through two little slots at the base of the window.

Delivery of newspapers, letters, the biannual Sears and Roebuck catalog, a spool of thread, a cut of tobacco all depended on R.F.D. mailmen, who brought daily contact with the outside world to isolated districts of the country.

Drawings were made from a R.F.D. mail wagon located in The Dalles, Oregon. The model was completed in 1941.

BAGGAGE AND TRANSFER TRUCK
1890-1920

Length: 54.0cm
Width: 26.5cm
Height: 29.5cm
Tongue: 40.5cm

OHS NEG. NO. OrHi 97262

This wagon was used during the heyday of American passenger trains, when most travel was done by rail. Hence, there were vast amounts of baggage and light freight to be hauled to and from the depots, and the baggage and transfer truck provided great service. In addition, heavier deliveries and the transfer of household furnishings were done by wagons of this type.

This one-and-a-half ton capacity, two-horse truck was operated in Eugene, Oregon. In the early 1940s Collins found it retired at the Eugene city stables.

Wartime shortages of materials delayed progress on the model, though Collins' requirements were limited. He finally mixed scraps of colors to complete it on September 30, 1945.

GOOSENECK DRAY
1895

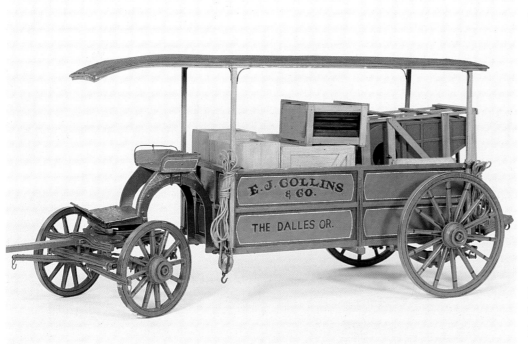

Length: 65.0cm
Width: 29.5cm
Height: 32.8cm

OHS NEG. NO. OrHi 97263

The gooseneck dray was named for the shape of the arch over its front hounds (this design allowed the front wheels to be turned sharply, making the wagon maneuverable in crowded warehouse and shipping areas). The dray's rear axle was underslung to place the bed of the wagon as close to the ground as possible, to facilitate loading.

Collins' father operated this wagon in 1895 for his general merchandising and freighting business in The Dalles, Oregon. Some years later, Collins found the wagon in Corvallis, Oregon and made drawings for the model, which he completed in 1939.

DRUMMER'S WAGON
1892

Length: 42.0cm   Height: 37.0cm
Width: 23.5cm   Tongue: 41.0cm

OHS NEG. NO. OrHi 97227

DRUMMER'S WAGON

Storekeepers in America's villages and small towns ordered their merchandise from "drummers," salesmen who traveled about the country carrying samples in these fancy wagons. Often, miniature versions of larger objects would be displayed, including beds, lamps, clocks, washing machines and irons—just about everything available. Today, these samples are highly valued as collectibles.

Collins made measurements and notes for the model from photographs. Further research by Collins indicated the running gear may have been built by Abbot-Downing and Co., the builders of the famous Concord coach, and the body and painting done by a local carriage smith at Nashua, New Hampshire.

The model was completed in 1941.

MEAT PACKER'S WAGON
ca. 1895

Length: 49.0cm
Width: 25.0cm
Height: 28.8cm
Tongue: 45.0cm

OHS NEG. NO. OrHi 97267

This was probably the most carefully designed and practical wagon of its type ever built. The spring system, fifth wheel assembly and "cut-under" front wheels, facilitated tight turns and gave this wagon a flexibility ideally suited to street and driving conditions of the horse-drawn era.

The Selle Gear Co. of Ohio developed and manufactured "running gear," or wheel, axle and spring assemblies, selling them as sub-assemblies to the wagon manufacturers.

The "sides of beef" inside the model are made from fabric that was stuffed, sewn and realistically painted!

While the model represents a particular wagon used by Armour and Co., this type of express vehicle was widely used for light trucking. In fact, Collins built the model as an express wagon in 1938, transforming it to Armour's meat wagon four years later. Today, wagons of this type are still used throughout the country for exhibition driving.

PHYSICIAN'S PHAETON
1884

Length: 55.5cm
Width: 20.0cm
Height: 27.5cm

OHS NEG. NO. OrHi 97270

Over 85,000 doctors would make house calls in horse-drawn carriages during the year this variation of the long-popular phaeton was designed.

One of its distinguishing features was the set of lockable drawers under the seat, which served as instrument case and private dispensary. The "close" top, extra-padded seat and high back afforded a doctor privacy and comfort during his round-the-clock schedule.

Drawings for this model, which was completed in 1965, were taken from the February 1, 1884 issue of *The Hub*, a trade journal for carriage and wagon manufacturers and enthusiasts.

MEDICINE WAGON
1885

Length: 50.0cm Height: 36.8cm
Width: 22.0cm Tongue: 30.5cm

MEDICINE WAGON

This is an exceptional example of the craftsmanship of carriage and wagon smiths. The exquisite carvings, even on partly hidden sections of the running gear, rivaled fine furniture and panel carving of the period.

The wagon was used by itinerant salesmen of patent medicine, whose products, often claimed to cure anything from snake bite to headache, were equally effective as furniture polish or harness oil.

To attract crowds and sales, salesmen staged entertainment—interspersed with the sales pitch—which varied from a single entertainer (with a wagon of this type) to a complete minstrel show (with bigger outfits). Many top-flight actors and musicians of yesteryear got their starts with the medicine shows.

The model, which was completed in January, 1942, is based on a wagon built by A. Miesner and Son of Sacramento, California.

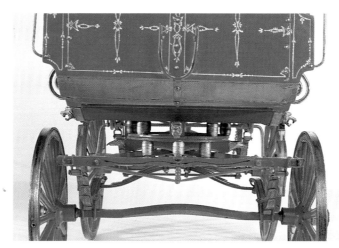

HANSOM CAB
1894

Length: 56.0cm
Width: 25.0cm
Height: 28.0cm

OHS NEG. NO. OrHi 97272

At the end of the horse-drawn age, the typical taxi was a Hansom cab. Passengers entered at the front and the driver, sitting roof-high at the back, received his directions through a trap door in the roof. The Hansom was named after its inventor, English architect Joseph Hansom, who patented the improved cab in 1835; the term "cab" is a contraction of the word *cabriolet*, an early two-wheeled public vehicle. Once frequenting many of the world's larger cities, the horse-drawn cabs still can be seen rolling through New York City's Central Park.

The model was completed in 1943, from a cab found in Alhambra, California, purchased in 1894 from J. A. Lawton and Co. of London and Liverpool.

HISTORIC VEHICLES IN MINIATURE
Industrial Wagons

LOGGING
WAGON
late 19th century

Length: 108.0cm
Width: 29.5cm
Height: 29.0cm

OHS NEG. NO. OrHi 97248

Many different kinds of wagons were used to haul logs through the woods to the mills. One of the best suited to the job, appearing in various forms throughout the Northwest, was this big solid-wheeled wagon. Usually ox-drawn, it cut down over the sidehill making its own road as it went; it could haul enough logs in one load to supply the lumber for a small house.

The unusual wheels, made from sections of large logs, were subject to shrinkage, cracking and checking. To compensate for this problem, the soft wood was driven full of oak pegs; after years of use and repair, the wheels resembled bundles of pegs.

The brake was operated by the sweep extending at the rear. The twelve-inch tread gave maximum braking surface and also permitted operation when the ground was soft in early spring. Collins completed this model in 1938.

WHEELED SCRAPER
ca. 1910

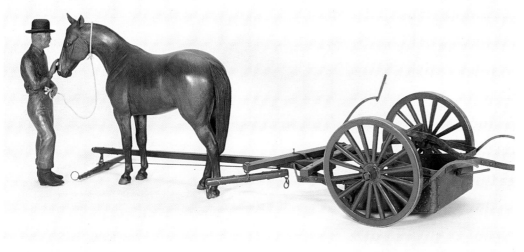

Length: 73.0cm
Width: 20.0cm
Height: 13.4cm

OHS NEG. NO. OrHi 97255

Before the big tractors and graders that do the job today, roads were built with machines and wagons pulled by horses or mules. One such contraption, the wheeled scraper, was loaded as it moved. A lever in the back lowered the scraper, which scooped up dirt. The load (up to three-fourths of a cubic yard) was then raised and dumped wherever necessary—to fill in the low places or to form long, railroad embankments.

Pulled by two or three horses, these scrapers were used regularly on highway and railroad fills as late as 1930, and in some areas considerably later.

Collins finished this model in 1947.

BOILER WAGON
1906

Length: 53.5cm
Width: 25.0cm
Height: 33.7cm
Tongue: 46.1cm

OHS NEG. NO. OrHi 97265

In 1906 this two-and-a-half ton, one hundred-horse-power boiler was hauled by six-horse team from Portland to Cedar Mill (roughly ten miles along an old wagon road with a graduated climb) for a new steam-powered sawmill. The driver sat astride the boiler, nine feet above ground. The heavy-duty, factory-built wagon was probably also used at the mill.

A half century earlier, the opening of western mines had played an important part in the development of the multi-million-dollar wagon freighting industry, a large portion of which was the hauling of engines, boilers and machinery. (In 1860, over 7,500 tons of machinery were freighted from the Missouri River to Colorado, a distance of over six hundred miles, all by team and wagon.)

The miniature boiler is actually made of riveted steel and contains over sixty-six feet of tubing for the flues; it weighs about 13 1/2 lbs (over 21 lbs with the wagon), and is fastened by about six hundred rivets. The model was designed after inspecting several boilers for details, and consultation with steam engineers.

The model wagon was drafted from a freight wagon at a Wasco County museum, and from reference to a Fish Brothers' wagon catalog. Wagon and boiler were both completed in 1968.

LOGGING CART
ca. 1912

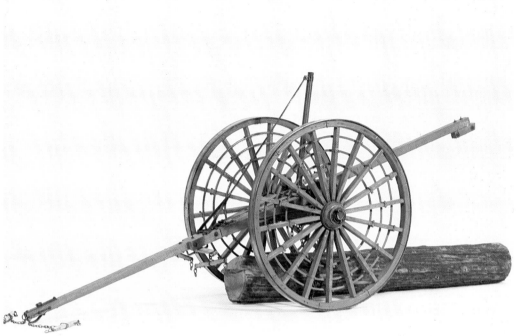

Length: 116.0cm
Width: 35.0cm
Height: 41.0cm

OHS NEG. NO. OrHi 97249

The immense wheels on this cart enabled it to straddle, lift (by means of the winch on the top) and move a load of logs. Horses, more easily maneuvered in the woods than oxen, were preferred for use with this type of rig.

The model, based on a logging cart that was originally used in Oregon's Coos Bay area, was completed in 1938.

OIL TANK WAGON
ca. 1914

Length: 53.0cm
Width: 27.5cm
Height: 37.3cm
Tongue: 41.2cm

OHS NEG. NO. OrHi 97264

Union Oil, Standard Oil and many other petroleum firms once hauled their products in horse-drawn tank wagons, carrying coal oil for lamps and stoves, and axle grease and machine oil to the livery stables for the conditioning of wagons and carriages. With the advent of the automobile, gasoline in increasing amounts was needed as well, so the tank was divided into three compartments of 165, 208 and 310 gallons, for oil, kerosene and gasoline, respectively. These compart-

ments were connected to faucets at the rear of the wagon. Axle grease was carried in a box on the back of the tank.

Wagons of this kind, and similar ones for water and sprinkling systems, were built by several manufacturers; the best known was Studebaker Brothers.

Collins made notes for the model, which was finished in 1944, from an oil tank wagon owned by 20th Century Fox.

STICK WAGON
SAND & GRAVEL WAGON
1850-1930

Length: 50.8cm
Width: 23.8cm
Height: 16.3cm
Tongue: 45.3cm

OHS NEG. NO. OrHi 97234

This model is based on one of the most common wagons used from about 1850 to the 1930s; the vehicle's design remained virtually unchanged during that period.

Loads of sand, gravel and dirt were dumped by simply prying up one of the side boards and turning over the two-by-fours on the bottom one at a time, spilling the load through the running gear. Reassembled in minutes, the wagon could quickly return for another load.

Collins did not consider the model complete until he let the body "age" in the weather during the winter of 1944-45.

HISTORIC VEHICLES IN MINIATURE
People-Mover Wagons & Sleighs

YELLOWSTONE
COACH
early 20th century

Length: 53.0cm
Width: 24.5cm
Height: 33.0cm
Tongue: 38.3cm

OHS NEG. NO. OrHi 97236

Another Abbot-Downing product was this sightseeing coach used in national parks. Like the famous Concords, the Yellowstone coach was slung on leather thorough-braces, and with crowding could carry twelve passengers.

In Yellowstone Park two hundred of these vehicles carried visitors and hotel guests on leisurely tours through the mountains. Four to six horses pulled each, and tourists returning year after year became almost as fond of favorite teams as of the scenery. A stock of two thousand horses was maintained to operate the Yellowstone coaches, replaced by motor buses in 1917.

Collins found the coach at Rancho El Providencia in Los Angeles, California, and spent two months constructing the model, which he completed on December 27, 1946.

WAGONETTE
1911

Length: 53.0cm
Width: 23.0cm
Height: 32.0cm
Tongue: 36.5cm

OHS NEG. NO. OrHi 97235

The ten-passenger carriage was popular with owners of large estates, serving as a sort of station wagon. Variations were used for public transportation, or could be hired at livery stables for use at picnics, funerals or group functions. Larger types were used as school buses.

The vehicle on which this model is based was built by McCabe-Powers Carriage Co. of St. Louis, Missouri. Refined design, thorough engineering and impeccable workmanship made this firm one of the top producers of fine horse-drawn vehicles. Still in business today,

the firm is a leading manufacturer of truck bodies and cranes for utility companies.

This wagonette was purchased in 1912 by Reginald H. Parsons, owner of Hillcrest Orchards in Medford, Oregon (it is still owned by the Parsons family). It transported women from Medford to the orchards to pack pears during the harvest season, August through October.

The model was completed in 1967.

TOP BUGGY
ca. 1900

Length: 33.8cm
Width: 21.8cm
Height: 28.0cm
Tongue: 32.5cm

OHS NEG. NO. OrHi 97271

The American buggy, whose general design evolved from an earlier pleasure wagon, became one of the most popular carriages of all time. It was a most ubiquitous vehicle, popular in both town and country for shopping, business and pleasure riding.

Numerous styles appeared, their names reflecting the design of the body or its suspension. One current source lists over twenty-five different names of buggies.

By 1916, the year in which automobile production finally surpassed wagon production, buggies were actually competing with the auto by advertising such features as electric lamps and an "automobile top."

Collins found this buggy in a stable in Culver City, California, and completed the model in 1941.

BREAK
ca. 1900

Length: 43.2cm
Width: 21.5cm
Height: 28.0cm
Tongue: 42.3cm

OHS NEG. NO. OrHi 97278

The ancestor of the break was a hunting phaeton with side-ventilated compartments for carrying dogs. Later, the vehicle was used for training and breaking horses, hence its name. Retaining its ventilator sides as ornaments, the break ultimately became popular as a sporting vehicle and for travel through rough countryside.

The original from which the model was drawn is now preserved at the Jacksonville Museum of Southern Oregon History in Jacksonville, Oregon. It was manufactured by E. M. Miller and Co. of Quincy, Illinois, around the turn of the century, and was used on the Rogue River summer estate of Nion Tucker. Collins completed the model in 1968.

BROUGHAM
1885

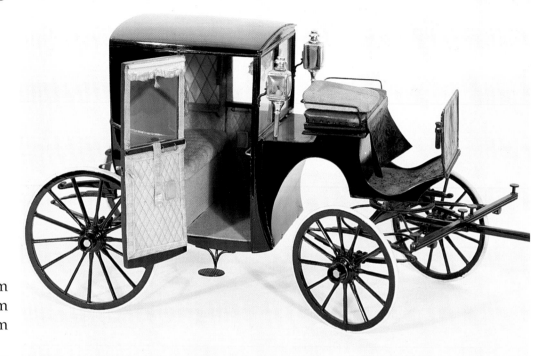

Length: 74.5cm
Width: 23.0cm
Height: 26.5cm

OHS NEG. NO. OrHi 97274

This coach was named in honor of London's Lord Brougham, who, in 1837, redesigned an existing type of closed carriage to fit his particular tastes and requirements. By the turn of the century it had become the most popular cab. Privately owned Broughams were driven by a coachman, with a footman in attendance alongside.

In addition to fine fabrics and upholstery, the interior usually included mirrors, calling-card cases, cigar cases, and, often, reading lamps. These appointments complemented the elegantly dressed ladies and gentlemen who rode in the Broughams.

The model was completed in 1941.

Length: 41.0cm
Width: 20.0cm
Height: 26.0cm

OHS NEG. NO. OrHi 97273

The Rockaway was not named for any characteristic sway. Rather, it was named for Rockaway, Long Island, by an unscrupulous sales firm that contrived to obtain exclusive dealership by misleading inquiries away from the actual manufacturer, who was in Jamaica, Long Island!

The Rockaway became particularly popular in democratic America, because the driver's seat was situated at passenger level. This enabled the head of a family to drive the carriage himself, rather than employ a driver to do it. Another popular feature was its extended roof, which protected the driver from the weather.

Collins made the model in 1950 from working drawings found in an 1883 issue of *Carriage Journal*.

BAROUCHE
1862

Length: 79.0cm
Width: 23.0cm
Height: 22.0cm

OHS NEG. NO. OrHi 97275

Just as we have borrowed many of our customs from foreign lands, so did the men who built American carriages borrow their designs and patterns. The prototype for this carriage came from France. Its real name was *caleche* but it came to be known in this country as a Barouche.

The barouche was America's favorite parade carriage. As many as six VIPs or officials could ride in one, waving or tipping their high silk hats along a parade route.

Many a president rode to his inauguration down the flag-draped streets of Washington, D.C. in this stately carriage.

Barouches incorporated an ingenious combination of springs and were built by the firm of T. E. Baldwin (1859-97); Baldwin had been a carriage designer with the famous firm of Brewster and Co.

Collins found the carriage at a stable in Burbank, California, and built the model in 1944.

VICTORIA
ca. 1890

Length: 88.0cm
Width: 20.5cm
Height: 23.7cm

OHS NEG. NO. OrHi 97276

The Victoria evolved from a type of carriage developed during the height of the French Empire. It was popularized by, and later named for, England's Queen Victoria (she enjoyed the fresh air and restful beauty of the parks, during her almost-daily drives in the open carriage).

The Victoria is an outstanding example of artistry and craftsmanship, possibly the most graceful vehicle ever designed.

This is the eleventh vehicle Collins built, and the first carriage he made. The model was completed in 1940.

PLEASURE WAGON
ca. 1825

Length: 31.8cm
Width: 21.5cm
Height: 18.5cm
Tongue: 25.2cm

OHS NEG. NO. OrHi 97281

Of the American rural vehicles marketed during the 18th century, the one brought most nearly to a state of perfection was the simple pleasure wagon. Its sweeping lines, the tasteful ornamentation of the rib-and-paneled body and sculptured structural parts of the running gear, gave this vehicle a simple grace and strength rarely duplicated.

The resemblance between the pleasure wagon and Conestoga wagon may be less coincidental than evolutionary; this pleasure wagon was America's first

family wagon, predating by 125 years the popular Surrey. Before elliptic springs came into use in the early 1800s, wooden springs, often consisting of only two wooden cantilevers, absorbed shock under the seats. Removable seats permitted use of the vehicle for hauling produce or supplies.

There are few pleasure wagons still around. Collins found this one at the Yakima Frontier Museum in Washington. Construction of the model was completed in September, 1969.

GOVERNESS CART
ca. 1885

Length: 42.0cm
Width: 21.5cm
Height: 22.0cm

OHS NEG. NO. OrHi 97280

The governess cart (larger versions were called tub carts) had a bench-like seat along each side, and a door at the back. As its name implies, the vehicle was driven by a governess, and was used chiefly to transport well-to-do children on their outings. The basket at the rear was for parasols.

The original of this cart was built by Laurie and Marner of Liverpool. Collins completed the model in 1941.

CANOPY-TOP SURREY
ca. 1910

Length: 37.0cm
Width: 22.0cm
Height: 28.8cm
Tongue: 42.5cm

OHS NEG. NO. OrHi 97279

Although the Surrey borrowed its name from a cart used in the County of Surrey, England, it was an American carriage built for American families, and it probably did more to unite scattered communities and families into a great nation of neighbors and friends than any other carriage or wagon. In 1910 this carriage could be purchased for about $85, and a double set Surrey harness for $21.

The model was completed in 1943 and is based on a Surrey found in a stable near Burbank, California.

BOBSLED
ca. 1915

Length: 92.0cm
Width: 16.5cm
Height: 23.8cm

OHS NEG. NO. OrHi 97238

Bobsleds were made in many styles and weights. The name comes from the bobbing up-and-down movement of the sled's runners. This is one of the heavier types, called a "knee bob." These sleds were constructed to support most wagon bodies for winter use. In the cities, delivery wagons and even fire-extinguishing apparatuses were mounted on bobsleds for winter operation.

Collins found this sled in Magna, Utah, and completed the model in 1945.

CUTTER
ca. 1870

Length: 48.8cm
Width: 14.5cm
Height: 14.3cm

OHS NEG. NO. OrHi 97241

In sleigh construction vehicle designers were at their best; without wheels or mechanical devices to constrict their fancy, they could execute the design in a harmony of gracefully flowing lines.

This type, often called a "swell cutter," because of its body's swelled sides, first appeared shortly after the Civil War.

The model is based on a cutter found in an antique shop in southern California. Collins did the drafting and built the model in less than two weeks in 1945.

SPRING SLEIGH
ca. 1905

Length: 23.8cm
Width: 13.8cm
Height: 17.5cm

OHS NEG. NO. OrHi 97239

The model is based on a spring sleigh built by Heinz Brothers of Menomonee Falls, Wisconsin, one of the first firms to incorporate what would seem to be an obvious improvement in sleighs—doors! Another advantage was its platform springs, added for increased comfort.

This sleigh belonged to Oregon Senator Wayne Morse. The senator was quite talkative and Collins had to ask his father to distract Morse with conversation while he did some quick drafting.

This is yet another model Collins completed in 1945, his most productive year.

ALBANY SLEIGH
ca. 1885

Length: 76.0cm
Width: 16.3cm
Height: 23.0cm

OHS NEG. NO. OrHi 97242

This model is based on a six-passenger sleigh made in the 1880s by the Albany, New York firm of Wemple and Pay.

In half-raised position, the folding top permitted passengers to view the snow-blanketed countryside while still providing some protection from cold winds. The flared leather wings protected them from chunks of ice and snow flying from the horses' hooves. The comfortable driver's cushion supported the coachman who handled four, and occasionally six, horses driven with this style of sleigh.

Around 1880, a sleigh of this type could be purchased for about $500; the price of four first-class horses and two sets of fine harness increased the investment from $1,000 to $4,000.

Collins made his model from an Albany sleigh found in Eugene, Oregon. This vehicle was destroyed in a fire shortly after Collins completed the model in 1967.

COLONIAL SLEIGH
ca. 1776

Length: 21.5cm
Width: 12.4cm
Height: 17.0cm

Single-horse sleighs like this one were entirely hand-made, with a minimum of ironwork. This particular sleigh has iron-shod runners, but many used only steamed hardwood, which was usually replaced at least once a season. The simple colonial sleigh contains some of the most graceful lines of any vehicle. Note the sweep of the body, reminiscent of the Conestoga wagon.

The year this model was completed, 1945, was by far Collins' most prolific year; he completed eight wagons and sleighs during that twelve-month period.

HISTORIC VEHICLES IN MINIATURE
War-Related Vehicles

CIVIL WAR CANNON AND LIMBER
1860-1865

Length: 55.8cm
Width: 25.0cm
Height: 19.3cm
Tongue: 45.9cm

OHS NEG. NO. OrHi 97243

Twelve-pounders were the mainstay of the Federal Field Artillery. During the war their range and accuracy were vastly increased with the introduction of rifling. These guns, with a five-degree elevation and a charge of two-and-one-half pounds of powder fired either solid or explosive shells, and had an effective range of 1,663 yards. In desperate situations they were often loaded with scrap iron and trace chains.

The second part of the unit, the limber, carried only enough ammunition to put the gun into action. Cannon and limber were pulled by four or six horses.

This model will fire a five-eighths-inch diameter solid shot using a half-thimbleful of powder and bears evidence of having seen action. Made in 1945, it represents one of the earlier smooth bores.

Length: 57.0cm
Width: 24.5cm
Height: 35.5cm
Tongue: 41.7cm

OHS NEG. NO. OrHi 97244

Thaddeus Lowe originated the idea of using balloons for observing and mapping the Confederate Army's movements. And it was Lowe who convinced President Lincoln of the need for the Balloon Corps.

Lowe's entire apparatus consisted of two generator wagons, each containing 650 pounds of iron filings and 800 pounds of sulphuric acid that produced hydrogen gas. The gas from the two wagons was hosed into a "cooler box" and then to a "washer box" and finally to the balloon. The two generators produced about twenty-thousand square feet of hydrogen gas, enough to inflate a balloon in about two hours. Aloft, Lowe telegraphed information to his ground crew, who held the balloon secure with lines.

Even today Lowe would be considered a "best-dressed" pilot, climbing into the gondola wearing his silk top hat and cut-away jacket!

Plans for the models were drafted from original drawings in the Smithsonian Institution. The two model wagons were completed in 1940.

ARMY ESCORT
WAGON, WWI
1918

Length: 45.0cm
Width: 24.0cm
Height: 25.3cm
Tongue: 44.8cm

OHS NEG. NO. OrHi 97245

This wagon, known as the standard four-mule escort wagon, had a load capacity of three-thousand pounds on good roads. Perfected and standardized during and immediately following the Spanish-American War, hundreds of these wagons were used to patrol the Mexican border and thousands were sent to France during World War I to accompany the combat train and carry rations and baggage.

The model was built in 1943 with measurements taken from a wagon built by the John Deere Plow Co. in 1918.

HISTORIC VEHICLES IN MINIATURE
How Ivan Collins Worked

Mrs. Laura Collins

Ivan's consuming passion was to preserve the history of horse-drawn transportation, to show how our people lived in that era. That his miniatures were also works of art was entirely beside the point—he could not work any other way.

He realized that these vehicles, being of perishable material, were fast disappearing, and he never went for a drive without keeping an eye out for the rotting remains of a wagon. When he found one (which became rarer in later years) he would ask the owner for permission to "draft" it. He would take his drawing equipment (later, his wife and then his daughters) and spend a day capturing every detail. Accuracy was his watchword. Nothing annoyed him more than the word "carve." These miniatures were not carved. They were built meticulously, exactly as the originals had been built. Even the placement of nails was noted on the drawings. Later, at home, he would convert these field drawings to shop drawings from which he made blueprints, and these he used to build the wagons.

All parts were completely operational—even the door latches worked. I remember that he spent one whole

Ivan Collins taking measurements for the express wagon in the 1940s. The completed wagon appears on p. 38.

OHS NEG. NO. **43325**

Ivan Collins spent many days in the field (literally) measuring actual wagons. Because of his tireless work, Collins rescued some important information, apparently in the nick of time. This dump wagon was built in miniature form by Collins in 1945.

OHS NEG. NO. **OrHi 35242**

Sunday experimenting with the weighting of the doors for the dump wagon so that they would come up precisely when operated by the winch, the left one coming up first and the right one just behind it so that it would overlap.

This construction was not a hobby—it was an obsession. Earning a living was secondary, and had to leave room for wagon building. When people would say, "I'd like to do something like that, but I don't have the time," he would say scornfully, "You don't *have* time, you *make* time." He would work evenings and weekends, and sometimes all night. When we were married [in 1944] he was working on the thirty-second model—the barouche. Before that, he would land in the hospital with exhaustion about once a year. After that, this never happened again, but I sometimes wondered when it would.

When things needed doing, he simply did them. For instance, he learned to tool leather in order to make the boot of the Concord coach authentic. And when he built the Umatilla House hotel omnibus and needed paintings above the windows (where today's buses have advertisements), he found that pictures in the right scale were simply not available, so he painted them.

Occasionally, remains of real wagons were not available. For example, the balloon gas generator wagons were not extant, having been destroyed in the retreat from Richmond during the Civil War (the War Department decided not to rebuild them, because "there is no value in aircraft"), so he acquired the drawings from the National Archives and built from them. The resultant miniature contains shelves of iron filings, over which hydrochloric acid could be poured to generate hydro-

HISTORIC VEHICLES IN MINIATURE

From the measurements that he had taken earlier, Ivan Collins drafts plans for the express wagon.

OHS NEG. NO. **OrHi 68052**

Ivan Collins in his workshop.

OHS NEG. NO. **OrHi 23854**

The Genius of Ivan Collins

Construction of the express wagon in Collins' workshop.

OHS NEG. NO. **OrHi 43329**

This 1941 photo shows Ivan Collins painting and attending to the final details of the road coach, which can be seen in its completed form on p. 5.

OHS NEG. NO. **OrHi 73460**

Collins patiently crafting the ironwork for the brewery wagon shown on p. 37.

These special tools are working on wheels that will eventually wind up on the express wagon.

The Genius of Ivan Collins

Ivan Collins enjoyed placing his wagons in natural settings and photographing them so that it was difficult to tell they were miniatures rather than the full-size wagon.

OHS NEG. NO. **OrHi 68053**

What appears to be a rest stop along a pioneer trail is actually Collins' Conestoga wagon, covered wagon, the buckboard, and their miniature accessories. This lifelike shot demonstrates this master model maker's painstaking attention to detail.

OHS NEG. NO. **OrHi 43371**

Here Collins carefully places an iron tire on a wooden wheel for one of his many fine models. The hub is secured to the scale-model workbench, the spokes are tapped into position and the felloes are fitted. Finally, a heated iron is attached to the wheel, and then is plunged into cold water to shrink the tire for a tight fit.

gen to fill the balloons. The problem, he always said, was to generate eighth-scale hydrogen. That one, he never licked. Hydrogen is hydrogen.

Later, after he learned what he was doing, he would sometimes build from the plans in a carriage builders' magazine—specifically the *Carriage Journal*, of which he acquired some originals and some reproductions.

His friend Don Hunter was a tremendous help to him. Don would take photographs of can and box labels and reduce them to the correct scale. (Don is as much a genius in his way as Ivan was in his.) Examples of these photographs are the labels on the boxes of apples on the orchard wagon, and labels on tin cans in the sheepherder's wagon.

When a wagon was completed and assembled, Ivan would completely disassemble it and apply lacquer—usually about eighteen coats, sanding between. I remember them so well—each piece attached to a wire and hanging from a line. I suppose that is the way the originals were painted. I always hated to see this happen to completed vehicles, but I knew that when this was all finished, the wagon would be assembled again, and would be beautiful. He insisted it was worth it, and of course it was.

Certain necessary tools were not available, so he made them: the spokeshave, the tire bender and the tire shrinker, for example. Only in this way could parts be built as they really were.

One of the storage cases that Ivan Collins designed to hold his wagons. He brought the same attention to detail to a storage container that he brought to his wagons. The container is brick red with yellow and black pin-striping on all sides.

OHS NEG. NO. **OrHi 97392**

Ivan Collins used this tool chest for the construction of many of his wagons. The tools, tiny screws, nails and bolts found in the tool chest were very useful during the restoration and cleaning of the wagons.
OHS NEG. NO. **OrHi 97391**

Wagons were always reproduced in their original form, so that those looking at them could see how they looked when they were new and people were actually using them.

How long did it take to build a wagon? Well, that depended, of course, on the wagon. The average was about six months. After he became creator and direc- tor of his own museum at the University of Oregon in 1965 and could work all the time, he turned them out faster. But he never completely finished, because there is no real end to this type of thing. When he died in 1971, our daughter placed in a glass case in the University museum a photograph of him at work, taken by Don Hunter, and the caption, "He left his work unfinished."

HISTORIC VEHICLES IN MINIATURE
Selected Plans

I van Collins rendered working drawings and selected plans for these remarkable miniature vehicles. The Oregon Historical Society Press offers 32 of these plans for sale. Their level of detail varies, depending on the plan, from exacting to basic elevation outlines. They were not originally intended for public use and are not engineered for full-size, road-safe vehicles. The originals of the plans reside in the Oregon Historical Society's Regional Research Library. On the following pages, you will see details from six of his plans.

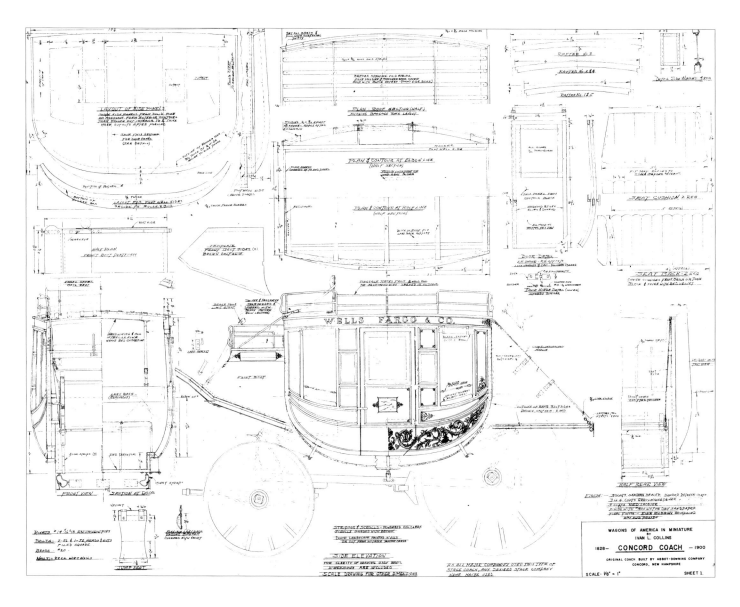

Concord Coach framing details (one sheet of a four-sheet plan)

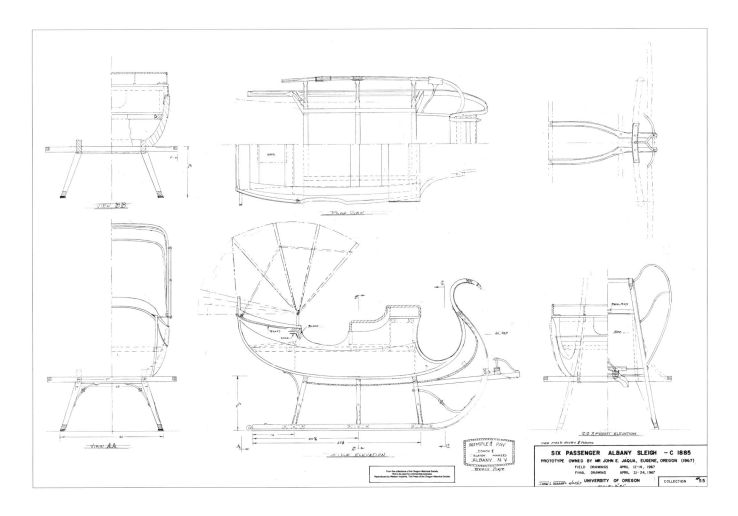

WEMPLE & PAY
COACH &
SLEIGH MAKERS
ALBANY N.Y.
BRASS PLATE

SIX PASSENGER ALBANY SLEIGH — C 1885
PROTOTYPE OWNED BY MR JOHN E. JAQUA, EUGENE, OREGON (1967)
FIELD DRAWINGS APRIL 12-14, 1967
FINAL DRAWING APRIL 21-24, 1967
UNIVERSITY OF OREGON
COLLECTION #55

Albany Sleigh

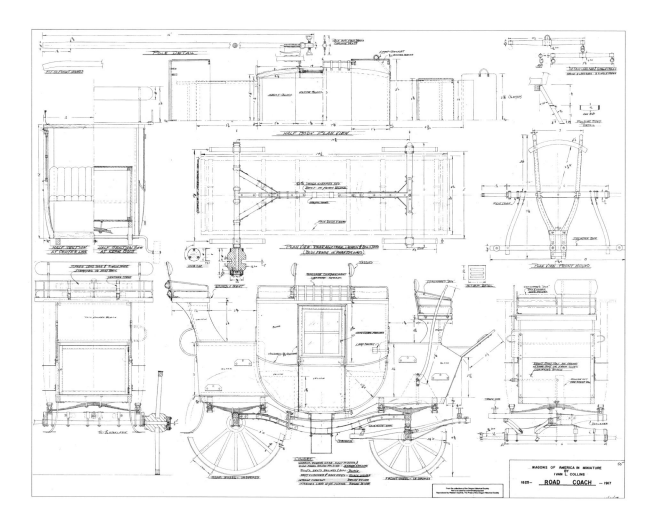

Road Coach

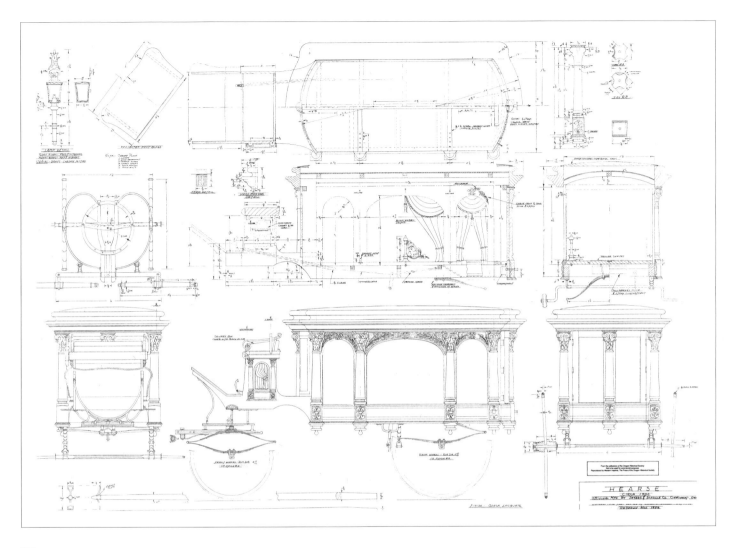

Hearse

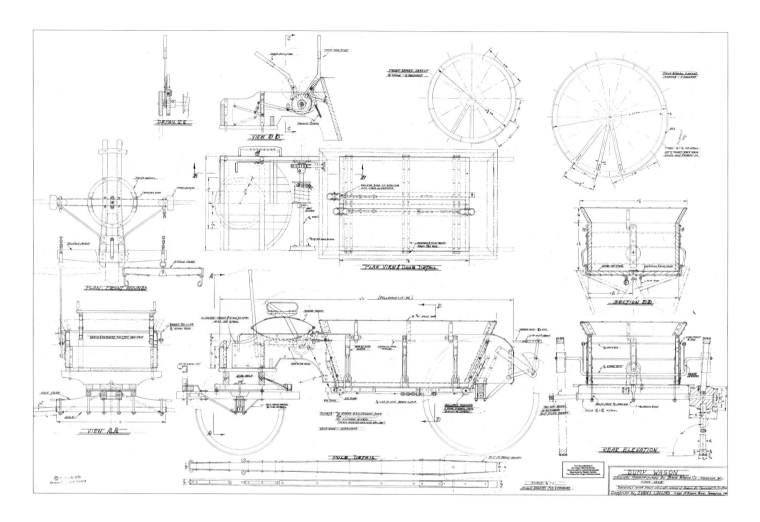

Dump Wagon

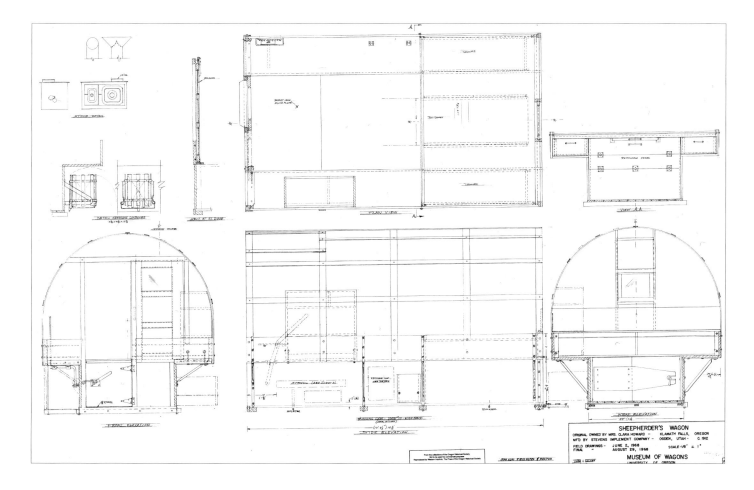

Sheepherder's Wagon

Ivan Collins' extant plans are preserved in the Manu-
script Collection of the Oregon Historical Society
Research Library.

HISTORIC VEHICLES IN MINIATURE
Selected Bibliography

Berkebile, Don H. *American Carriages, Sleighs, Sulkies, and Carts*. New York, 1977.

———. *Carriage Terminology: An Historical Dictionary*. Washington, D.C., 1978.

Carlisle, Lilian B. *The Carriages at Shelburne Museum*. Shelburne, Vt., 1956.

The Carriage Journal. Carriage Association of America.

Collins, Ivan L. *Horse Power Days*. Stanford, Ca., 1953.

Florin, Lambert. *Western Wagon Wheels*. New York, 1970.

G. and D. Cook and Co.s *Illustrated Catalogue of Carriages and Special Business Advertiser*. [New Haven, Conn.] 1860. (Reprint. New York, 1974).

Gannon, William L. "Carriage, Coach and Wagon," Ph.D. dissertation, State University of Iowa, 1960.

Rittenhouse, Jack D. *American Horse-Drawn Vehicles*. Los Angeles, 1951.

Rose, Albert C. *Historic American Roads*. New York, 1976.

Thompson, John. *Making Model Horse-Drawn Vehicles*. Fleet, Hampshire, U.K. n.d.

1939-1997

RON BRENTANO

While the book *Historic Vehicles in Miniature* celebrates the obvious genius of Ivan Collins, the Oregon Historical Society would like to take a page to celebrate the less visible genius of our co-worker and friend, the late Ron Brentano. Ron came to the Oregon Historical Society in 1969. Through his work as Curator of Technology and later as Chief Field Representative, he cast a warm and enthusiastic eye on the many manifestations of Oregon history.

It was through Ron's enthusiasm for technology in its varied guises that the Ivan Collins Collection came to the Oregon Historical Society. Ron did the primary research on the details of the wagons and wrote the text for this catalog. Prior to his death from cancer, he was able to appreciate the glowing details of these beautifully restored wagons. We miss his abundant good humor and his sheer pleasure in Oregon's history, but we see a bright piece of it reflected in this book.

Colophon

Historic Vehicles in Miniature is printed on 80-lb. Somerset. The typeface Palatino is used throughout this volume. Palatino was designed by Hermann Zapf for the Stempel foundry in 1950. It is one of the most widely used typefaces in the world today. Its classical Italian Renaissance letterforms blend with the crispness of line needed for 20th-century printing processes, and Palatino's generous width aids readability at small sizes.

This volume was produced and designed by the Oregon Historical Society Press.

Production of this work was achieved through the expertise and cooperation of the following:

Photography: Maurice Hodge, Evan Schneider

Interior design, typesetting, & layout: Lori McEldowney

Cover design: K-P Design • Portland, OR

Scanning: Precision Digital Imaging • Tigard, OR

Printing: Paramount Graphics • Beaverton, OR